Victoria with Kids
By Lhasa Hetherington
Copyright 2014 Lhasa
Hetherington
ISBN 978-0-9937239-1-9

Contents

Victoria with Kids

Victoria is a wonderfully kid friendly city. There is everything a kid (and a parent) could want here. Downtown is extremely walkable and has some very charming old buildings and squares. Then there is the Inner Harbor, where you can spy ships and boats, helicopters and sea planes, all busy at work. There are museums and attractions that your children will get a kick out of, as well as plenty of shopping, both for the kids and the adults. Victoria has a thriving dining scene that, for the most part, is kid friendly, and offers many delicious choices.

If you take a step off the beaten path and explore the neighborhoods surrounding downtown you will find many more things to do. Beaches, shopping, playgrounds and parks, and of course good eating!

Victoria is small enough to see everything with ease. At a relaxed pace, you can certainly fit activities in around a little one's naps. Be it a neighborhood walk, a playground and beach adventure, or a visit to the museum and a quick lunch.

Most every neighborhood in Victoria has a little shopping street- that is just a few blocks long, making it manageable with children in tow. Most have a children's boutique or toy store, and most have some nice adult shopping! Not to mention a café or bakery where you can take a quick break and re-charge with something tasty.

Throughout this book I'll shine a light on the toy and clothing stores that are really worth poking around in. I'll also share with you the amazing restaurants that are dotted around the city and neighborhoods. There are some really good ones.

I know from experience that the best days my family has traveling are centered around a great activity for the kids, so I will let you in on each neighborhood's best places to play. Don't worry; there will always be a coffee shop close

• WHERE TO STAY

While there are plenty of great hotels in Victoria, I lean towards, and have always had great experiences renting places on air bnb, or another reputable vacation rental site. I find the benefits when traveling with children are immense. For one, there is always more space. There is always a kitchen so you don't have to eat every meal out. If you pick your place right it will come furnished with toys and baby necessities. Plus you will really get to see some areas of the city you might not see otherwise.

Here are some considerations when choosing a home to rent:
- How close is it to a grocery store
- Is parking easy
- How many bedrooms
- Will you have access to a crib and/or any other baby supplies
- Is it in a noisy area
- Will it be easy to get your stroller in and out
- Are there playgrounds and shops nearby
- Is the place you are renting the owner's primary residence

If this is something that concerns you, you might be better off using a Vacation Rental site rather than air bnb.

There are some great neighborhoods in Victoria that are close enough to downtown, yet offer a quieter atmosphere and great family amenities. I will go into detail on these neighborhoods further along the book. But know for now, that if you book a place in any of the following locations you will be no more then 10 minutes from the downtown core and there will be some great things to do close to your front door.
- Fernwood
- Oak Bay
- Fairfield
- James Bay
- Vic West

If you go the hotel route, most good hotels are located in the downtown core. I find booking a hotel with an indoor pool is a real plus, as it gives the kids something to do at home base.

If you can afford it, try to get a suite. This way when the kids go to bed you don't need to sit in the dark watching them sleep!

• GETTING AROUND

Victoria has an adequate transit system, though not as good as other places. Busses can come infrequently, and routes may not take you exactly where you want to go. If you have to rely on it then you will be a little limited, but should be able to make things work. However, if you have a car it will afford you a lot more flexibility and freedom, especially when it comes to exploring the outlying areas, or if you want to experience some good old west coast nature.

In Canada, car seats are required by law unless you are using public transportation, which for some reason means that while driving a rental car you need a car seat, but while riding in a taxi (or on a bus) you do not.

When driving here keep in mind a few Victoria foibles:
- Many of the streets here change names at some point. For example, Cook Street turns into Maplewood Street and then later turns into Blenkinsop. So keep a close eye on your map when driving.
- Parking downtown is usually no problem. Park and then look for the blue ticket kiosks. Once you pay, you will get a receipt that does not need to be put in the car. Keep this with you so know when your time is out!
- Parking regulations are strictly enforced. If you are haphazard about putting money in the meter you will get a ticket. Also note that there are time restrictions for street parking, usually 90 minutes. If you plan to be longer then this, look for a parking lot, or a parkade. There are a few of these sprinkled through the downtown core.
- You do not need to pay for parking before 9am, after 6pm or all day Sundays and Holidays.
- If you can avoid going to The Westshore (Colwood or Langford) between 3 and 5, do so. The traffic gets really really backed up on the highway and it can take a long time to get there. (this is known as 'The Colwood Crawl')

8

• GETTING SUPPLIES

Most neighborhoods have a grocery store, which you can get not only food, but also diapers and baby supplies. Most will have pharmacies in them as well (but not all). All stores are noted at the beginning of each neighborhood chapter.

If you are staying right downtown, your best bet is The Market on Yates, in the Harris Green Plaza (Yates Street at Quadra). Also in the plaza is a London Drugs, where you can get baby supplies and a pharmacy if necessary. If you feel like a bottle of wine (and you just might)… note that our grocery stores do not sell any alcohol. You will need to go to either a cold beer and wine, or government liquor store.

If you are looking to rent baby gear there are two companies that do this:

Abra-kid-abra
http://www.abra-kid-abra.com/

Wee Travel
http://www.weetravel.ca/

• CLINICS & HOSPITALS

In Canada, pharmacists are not permitted to write prescriptions. In the event that you need to get a prescription written you will need to visit a doctor and then go to the pharmacy to get it filled. If you need medical assistance there are a few walk-in clinics, usually one in every neighborhood.

Hospitals

If you need emergency assistance you will need to get to a Hospital. Victoria uses the 911 system if you are unable to drive.

Victoria is served by two hospitals:

The Royal Jubilee (in Oak Bay)
1952 Bay Street
(250) 370-8000

Victoria General (in View Royal)
1 Hospital Way
(250) 727-4212

Walk In Clinics

Downtown
Downtown Medical Clinic
622 Courtney Street, 250 380 2210

Yates & Quadra Integrated Health Center (in the Harris Green Center)
105-911 Yates Street, 250 388 3080

Fairfield
Cook Street Village Walk In Medical Clinic
230 Cook Street, 250 220-9999

10

Oak Bay
Jubilee Medical Clinic
1902 Richmond Road, 250 592 3441

Oak Bay Medical Clinic
101-1640 Oak Bay Avenue, 250 598 6744

24 hour Pharmacy- Shoppers Drug Mart in UpTown
Shopping Center
3511 Blanshard Street Avenue, 250 475 7572

• RAINY DAYS

Rain got you down? Don't worry; there are plenty of things for families to do here.
For young children, Playgroups are a good way to go (see write up in subsequent chapter).
Many of Victoria's Touristy Things are in-doors and will get you out of the drizzle.

Good for a rainy day are:
The Royal BC Museum
Bug Zoo
Maritime Museum
Miniature World

There are also some indoor play areas. Tumblebums and The Playzone (look in The Westshore Chapter for information).

Our libraries offer a weekly drop in story time and have a good little kid's area. Check out gvpl.ca for times.

We have a great selection of rec-centers- they offer drop-in swimming, ice skating, tennis, kindergyms and more. Have a browse on each rec-center site to see what they offer and if the timing works for you.

Oak Bay Rec Center
https://www.oakbay.ca/parks-recreation/facilities-rentals/recreation-centres/oak-bay-recreation-centre
swimming, ice skating, tennis

Esquimalt Rec Center
http://www.esquimalt.ca/parksRecreation/
Swimming, kindergym

Pearkes Arena
http://www.saanich.ca/parkrec../recreation/pearkes.
html
Ice Skating, playgroups

Saanich Commonwealth Pool
http://www.saanich.ca/parkrec../recreation/
commonwealth.html
Swimming

Movie Theathers

Or try a movie, both of the SilverCity theaters offer
Stars and Strollers- which are special screenings where
you can bring your younger babies. Check their website
for more details. We find the Imax, at the Royal BC
Museum, works well with our five year old, as the
movies are around 45 minutes long, which is the perfect
amount of time for a young child.

Imax
675 Belleville Street (at the Royal BC Museum)
250 480 4887, www.imaxvictoria.com

Odeon- Downtown Location
780 Yates Street, 250 383 0513, http://www.cineplex.
com/Theatres/TheatreDetails/Cineplex-Odeon-Victoria-
Cinemas.aspx

SilverCity
Tillicum Mall Area, 3130 Tillicum Road, 250 381 9301
http://www.cineplex.com/Theatres/TheatreDetails/
SilverCity-Victoria-Cinemas.aspx

SilverCity
Westshore Location, 900 2945 Jacklin Rd, 250
474 1007 http://www.cineplex.com/Theatres/
TheatreDetails/Cineplex-Odeon-Westshore-Cinemas.
aspx

• PLAYGROUPS

Playgroups are a great way for young children to have a lot of fun and for you to meet some local parents (who will have more tips on fun kid friendly things to do). Victoria has quite a few of them. As times and days change frequently, please check each website for times and days. The best, in my experience, are listed below.

Fairfield Community Center
1330 Fairfield Road, 250 382 4604
www.fairfieldcommunity.ca/programs/dropin.html
They offer 2 drop in's; parent & tot (birth to 5), by donation
and kindergym, (walking -5), $2
Both fill up quickly so be there a few minutes early to ensure you get in!

James Bay Community Center
140 Oswego Street, 250 389 1470
www.jamesbaycentre.ca/programs/early-childhood
Kindergym, Birth-5, $4

Victoria YMCA
851 Broughton Street, 250 386 7511
http://www.victoriay.com/schedules.php
The Y is right downtown, and offers some drop-ins on Saturday mornings. The website is a bit hard to navigate, on the right hand side of the page you will see a blue box with drop-in schedules, click on 'child' to see what they have.

Saanich Rec Centers
Various locations
www.saanich.ca/parkrec../recreation/dropin/index.html

Pearkes, Gordon Head, and Saanich Commonwealth all offer drop in Kindergym.
To find information scroll to the bottom of page and click on Drop In Kindergym.
If the Pearkes Kindergym fit's into your day, it is located right behind Tillicum Mall, which is home to Old Navy, Winners, and Target...so you can combine your kindergym with a little shopping!

Henderson Rec Center
2291 Cedar Hill X Road, 250 370 7200
www.oakbay.ca/parks-recreation/programs/kindergym
Located in deep Oak Bay, this is a good sized kindergym, lots of ride 'ems and sports stuff, and sometimes a bouncy castle. Usually they fill up so it's good to go early to ensure a spot.

Mothering Touch
975 Fort Street, 250 595 4905
http://www.motheringtouch.ca/
Mothering Touch offers a few drop ins:
Yoga, Stretch and Dance, Sing and Sign, Fun in French, Toddler Yoga and more.
Check there web-site for more information!

Fernwood Community Center
1240 Gladstone Avenue, 250 381 1552
http://fernwoodnrg.ca/neighbourhood/fernwood-community-centre/
This playgroup is held in the gym which gives kids plenty of room to run around and act crazy!

• CLASSES

If you are looking for a fun class to do with you child, you can check out these options. A little more planning in advance needs to happen, as you have to pre-register and space can fill up. But if you get it together to get into one of these classes, you and your children will have a lot of fun and have a great memory to take home.

The London Chef
953 Fort Street, 250 590 1865
http://thelondonchef.com
You and your kids will love these totally engaging cooking classes. Chef Dan Hayes does a wonderful job teaching children (and you) about food and cooking. At the end all the kids get to sit down and enjoy the fruits of their labour.

4 Cats Art Studio
http://www.4cats.com/oakbay
http://www.4cats.com/langford
http://www.4cats.com/cordovabay

This is a great place to get creative. Your children will leave with a neat piece of art and some new skills. There are 3 locations in Victoria. Each will have a different schedule, so make sure you check them each out if you are looking for an art class.

The Paint Box
http://www.thepaintbox-victoria.com
A few minutes from Downtown, tucked away in Fernwood, The Paint Box is another great place to make art. They have 1 day workshops for all age groups and the kids make really unique and interesting projects.

The Victoria Public Market
http://victoriapublicmarket.com
From time to time there are kid's programs (cooking related) on Saturdays between 1-3 in the community kitchen at The Victoria Public Market. Check out their website, as it seems to be a little unpredictable.

• SHOPPING

Victoria has some pretty great shopping. If you prefer independent boutique shopping, check out lower Johnson Street (between Broad and Wharf Street), there are some cool clothing boutiques. Fort Street between Cook and Vancouver has some nice shops too, mainly antiques, clothing, and a ton of yoga studios. Government Street is the main tourist drag and this is where you will find all your Victoria T-Shirts and trinkets. For children's shopping please refer to the neighborhood guide.

In addition there are five malls, each with their own highlights.

Mayfair Mall
3147 Douglas Street
http://www.mayfairshoppingcentre.com/
A 10 minute drive from downtown, in my opinion the best mall in Victoria- a good selection of non-kid shopping, and for the kids, Toy's R Us- there is also a Gap, and a Gymboree.

Hillside Center
1644 Hillside Avenue, http://hillsidecentre.com/
The future home of Target- opening in the Spring of 2014. This mall is undergoing major renovations right now, and is starting to look great; however the selection of shops is not that impressive.
The exception is Bolen Books, which is a fantastic book store for both kids and adults.
There is a Thrifty Foods and a Shoppers Drug Mart in this mall as well.

Uptown Shopping Center
At the Intersection of Douglas or Blanshard and Saanich Rd http://www.shopuptown.ca/
Home of H&M, Forever 21, Future Shop, Joe Fresh, Wal-mart and more. This is an open air mall, and there is a courtyard in front of Wal-Mart that is a good place to take a shopping break and let the kids run around.
Victoria's only 24 hour pharmacy is located here at the Shoppers Drug Mart.

Tillicum Center
3170 Tillicum Rd, http://www.tillicumcentre.ca
The major draw of Tillicum Center is Target, Winners, and Old Navy. There is a Safeway here as well as a London Drugs. Behind the mall is SilverCity Movie Theater and Pearkes Rec Center.

The Bay Center
1150 Douglas Street, http://www.thebaycentre.ca/en
There is not much shopping for the kids in the mall downtown. There are washrooms with change tables and a nursing area. There is a food court on the top level that has a pretty decent selection of quick food. The Bay department store is here as well as Scallywags (on the Fort Street side).

• NATURE WALKS

Victoria and the surrounding areas have some pretty breathtaking scenery; with a short drive you can see some of our lush forests, still serene lakes, or rocky brambly shorelines.

Thetis Lake
http://www.crd.bc.ca/parks/thetis/

Thetis Lake is off of the Trans Canada Highway. Take the Colwood exit following the Island Highway. Turn right on Six Mile Road, which leads to the park entrance.

Thetis is around a 20 minute drive from downtown, depending on traffic. If you are leaving Victoria between 3 and 6 you will get stuck in the dreaded 'Colwood Crawl', which is not where you want to be. It is Victoria's version of a New York traffic jam, and will add a lot of extra travel time.

Parking is free at Thetis Lake from October to April. Pay parking is in effect from May 1 to September 30, and in the summer the lot can be quite full.

Once at the lake you will see a public beach directly behind the parking lot- just follow the signs. It is shallow and sandy (if not crowded with teenagers on a hot summer day).

There are trails that will take you around the lake, where you will be surrounded by pines and arbutus trees, and in the spring little wild flowers poking their heads out.

It takes over an hour to get around the lake, so know your crowd. If you have a good sturdy 3 wheel stroller you will make it, if not, choose a different form of toting. If you have little kids you can just walk and explore for a bit and then turn around.

Swan Lake
http://www.swanlake.bc.ca/

Swan Lake is an impressive park. There is a real diversity of sites. Marshy areas give way to the forest, which then gives way to open and wild grassy fields. There are swans, many different varieties of ducks, and other wildlife to be spotted.

The Nature House, by the parking lot, is the information centre for the Swan Lake. Check out the interpretive displays, discover nature hands-on and up-close, visit the live bee "house" and browse the natural history reading room....once out on the trail you get pretty fields, quite wooded areas, boardwalks over marsh, herons, ducks, and more.

It is a long walk all the way around...I wouldn't attempt it with smaller children. If you have little guys with you, you can head down from the nature hut and stay right, in a few minutes you will get to the boardwalk over the marshes which is pretty fun. Then just turn around and head back the way you came. If your kids are older and have more stamina take them around the whole lake. It's around an hour and is not stroller friendly.

Swan Lake offers Nature Classes as well. They are around 2 hours long and cover a variety of topics about the surrounding natural flora and fauna, but you must pre-register, so check their website for more information.

Swan Lake is around 15 minutes from downtown by car: By Car: (From Downtown Victoria) Go North on Blanshard Street. (Pat Bay Highway #17) and take the McKenzie Avenue exit, right on Rainbow Street., left on Ralph Street., right on Swan Lake Road. The parking lot entrance is on the left.

Mount Douglas Park

Mount Douglas has a few things going for it and is a pretty diverse area to explore. There are the shores of Cordova Bay, and then there is the surrounding forest. With older children you can hike from the beach through the fir trees and ferns and up to the summit of the mountain. The trails here can be steep in parts, so use caution.

This 360º lookout is spectacular, with views of rural Saanich, city lights of Victoria, and further, the Olympic and Cascade mountains in Washington State.

You can also choose to drive up to the top- which is a good way to go with the little ones.

Or, if the beach is more your style, Mount Douglas Park beach is a long sandy beach and can be accessed via trail off the main parking lot near the Shelbourne/Ash intersection. Washrooms and playground are off main parking lot also. This area is not stroller friendly.

If you have outdoorsy kids this is a great place to spend some time. Pack in food and water as there is no concession.

Elk & Beaver Lake

Elk Lake is a favorite Victoria swimming hole in the summer. It is around 20 minutes from downtown (you pass it on the way in from the ferry) by car.

Eagle Beach is at the northern part of the lake. Here you can swim, play at the playground, picnic at the tables and just enjoy the day. It is quite shallow at the shoreline, so it is suitable for very little ones to splash safely around. You will see people floating around the lake in inflatables, which can be a fun thing to do with your older kids. There are no inflatable sales offered here though, so bring your own.

Beaver Lake is the southern part of the lake, and has a sandy beach (not quite as nice as elk lake though), and a playground.

There are also easy hiking trails around both lakes- which is manageable if you have a
sturdy 3 wheeled stroller.

There is no concession here, so bring your own food and water!

Beaver Lake Entrance
Follow the Pat Bay Highway from Victoria, and take the Royal Oak Drive exit. Turn left on Royal Oak Drive to cross over the highway, then right on Elk Lake Drive to reach the park entrance on the left.

Elk Lake Entrance
Follow the Pat Bay Highway from Victoria. Turn left on Sayward Road, left again on Hamsterly Road, then right on Brookleigh Road, which leads to the park entrance on the left.

Cuthbert Holmes Park
The entrance is located at the far end of the parking lot behind Tillicum Mall (close to The SilverCity)
The park itself is a small system of hard packed trails and little bridges that meander through a nice wooded area, and eventually end up following the shores of Colquitz Creek. This is a great park with little ones, as it not a strenuous walk, is stroller friendly, and it is close to town (and shopping at the mall).

Esquimalt Kinsman Gorge Park
On Tillicum Road between Craigflower and Gorge Rd.
Esquimalt Gorge Park is not as nature driven as say Swan Lake, but there is a nice paved (stroller friendly) walkway along the Gorge, and it's close to town. There is a good playground here- as well as lots of bird life.
There is also a big grassy field, picnic tables and a washroom, if you wish to have a lunch here.

• BEACHES

Victoria has a nice mix of sandy and rocky beaches. Sandy beaches offer a nice place to build castles and dig your toes in, and the rocky beaches give kids an opportunity to comb the beach for cool rocks, launch drift wood boats, and generally muck about.

I have mentioned the beaches that are in our neighborhoods in each chapter, but you can click on the links here to see them: Cadboro Bay Beach, Gonzales, The Rock Beach, and Willows Beach.

The following beaches are on the outskirts of Victoria & are worth the drive if time permits.

Esquimalt Lagoon
http://www.esquimaltlagoon.com/

Located in Metchosin, Esquimalt Lagoon is around a 25 minute drive from downtown.

Esqimalt Lagoon is a neat little bay with one side of the road a migratory bird sanctuary and the other side a pebbly beach that stretches on for quite a ways. There is an old bridge and some sand bars to explore. From here you have a view of the Esquimalt dock yards.

We sometimes risk taking the kids to the box stores in Langford, in turn rewarding them with a stop here on the way home.

Witty's Lagoon
http://www.wittyslagoon.com/

Further into Metchosin is Witty's Lagoon. You will be treated to some beautiful country views on the 40 minute drive from town.

We love Witty's Lagoon! Usually there are not too many people here, the beach is gorgeous white sand, and the water is so shallow you can safely wade out quite far. We usually pack a picnic and spend the day, as Witty's is not close to town.

From the main parking lot off of Witty Beach Road, where you will find the nature center, it is around a 20-30 minute walk to the beach area through a typical lush West Coast rain forest, complete with marshy areas and plenty of bird life. This path isn't particularly stroller friendly so a back-pack or carrier is a good idea.

The beach here is amazing. It is a super shallow long sandy lagoon, so even the littlest of kids can go for a safe splash here. Because it is so shallow, on hot days the water warms up a tiny bit- making it more tolerable than most places.

If you aren't up for the forest walk, but still want to enjoy the beach you can come in on the Tower Point Entrance. To reach Tower Point, turn off of Metchosin Rd and follow Duke Road to Olympic View Drive. From the parking lot head towards the water and you will walk down a long wooden staircase which will deposit you directly across from the sandy stretch of beach. You will have to be prepared to walk through the water to get to the beach though...if the tide is high, it can come up to knee level on an adult so small children will have to be carried. I would not recommend this in the colder months for obvious reasons!

There are washrooms at the head to each trail; however the beach area offers washrooms, so you will have to be resourceful!

• TOURISTY THINGS

There is a whack of touristy things to do in Victoria, most of it is good fun, but, touristy. The following seem to be destinations that kids like best. Often if you keep your eye on Groupon, Couvon, or Island Daily Deals you will find discounts for some of these. If you come to Victoria in late February /early March, check out Be a Tourist in Your Hometown for more deals.

Craigdarroch Castle
http://thecastle.ca
Just off Fort Street at 1050 Joan Crescent, with parking available on site and along the street where indicated.
This is a neat place to go stomp around. Don't schedule too much time for the castle visit, as it won't take long to buzz through it, especially if your kids are small!
Keep an eye out for ghosts, rumor has it there are a couple that haunt the castle!
From the Castle you can either check out Fernwood, Oak Bay or Fairfield, as those neighborhoods are within a few minutes of the Castle.

Harbour Ferries
http://www.victoriaharbourferry.com/
Various locations and prices.
These little boats are great fun for kids! There is an assortment of tours and destinations you can choose from, ranging from around 15 minutes to well over an hour- which is great, as you can choose a short route if you are with smaller children who bore easily! They will let you fold up your stroller and take it on the boat, so you can use the ferries as a mode of transportation rather then just a tour. For instance you can hop on downtown and hop off at Fisherman's Wharf.

Royal BC Museum
675 Belleville Street
http://royalbcmuseum.bc.ca

The Royal BC Museum is well worth it! Depending on the age of your kids of course this can be anywhere from a ½ hour trip to a ½ day trip. There is ton's to see. There are amazing exhibits and galleries of all things BC.

Walk through the rain forests and spy the moose and bear, then make your way to the wild West Coast and take in the sea lions basking in the sun. Tour wet lands, walk in an old mine, or pan for gold. Your kids can run wild in Old Town, up and down the stairs of the old hotel. Surely someone is making apple pie? How about the famous woolly mammoth who reigns large and fierce?

There is a ton of First Nations artifacts and totem poles as well as a really neat pit house that depicts how our Fist People lived hundreds of years ago. It's pretty awesome!

There is a little café on site where you can get snacks or lunch. If you pack a lunch there are benches outside the exhibits on the second floor where you can eek out a spot and enjoy the views of the harbour.

Most of the exhibits are stroller friendly. There are some stairs though. If you are comfortable with it, park your stroller at the bottom of the stairs, and go walk though the exhibit and then come back for your stroller.

There is a gift shop which has a great selection of educational toys and books.

This is a must see!

Maritime Museum
28 Bastion Sq, http://mmbc.bc.ca/
The Maritime Museum houses fascinating displays on pirates, heritage vessels, shipwrecks and featured exhibits. It is also home to three significant sailboats – Dorothy,Trekka and Tilikum – each with their own incredible story of adventure and enchantment.

There are lots of model ships, and a really cool creaky old birdcage elevator that will take you to the top floor where there is a restored courtroom. The judge that used to preside over this court was known as 'The Hanging Judge', and it is rumored that the little knotted tree in Bastion Square is where the hangings took place. It's a bit random, but kind of neat.

This is not a big museum and it doesn't take long to breeze through. It would entertain a nautical buff for at least a short spell.

It is right in Bastion Square, which is a pleasant place to have a coffee and snack afterwards.

Most of the Maritime Museum is stroller friendly.

Miniature World
649 Humboldt Street, 250 385 9731, in the bottom of the Empress Hotel
http://www.miniatureworld.com/
Adult's $12, Youth $10, Child $8- ask about the family rate
While a little cheesy and touristy, kids love Miniature World. They will be plunged into deep space upon entrance, only to come out to witness old time Canada, complete with the great Canadian railway, a miniature working train (which your kids can control with the push of a button).

Then move into the Wild West and Frontier Land. After that you can marvel at Fantasy Land. Finally in the last exhibit is a room of intricate doll houses…almost each one has some sort of switch that kids love to turn off and on to see what will happen.

This is also a must in my opinion (do it for the kids)!

This is a stroller friendly event.

Hippo Ride
468 Belleville Street, 250 590 5290
http://www.victoriahippotours.com/
Only April through October, tickets are a steep $48 for an adult, $28 for those 3-12, and $5 for a toddler.
If you are going to do a bus tour this is the one to do. It is a 90 minute ride, 50 are spent on land, and then your hippo bus will make a dive into the ocean, where the remaining 40 minutes will be spent viewing Victoria from the sea.

Bug Zoo
631 Courtney Street, 250 384 2847
http://www.bugzoo.bc.ca/
2 and under free, 3-10 $7, 11-18 $8, adults $10
The Bug Zoo hosts an amazing world of insects and spiders. A visit to the bug zoo offers visitors an excellent opportunity to view and experience multi-legged creatures from around the world in a safe, fun and friendly atmosphere. Get up close and personal with LIVE giant walkingsticks, alien-eyed praying mantids, hairy tarantulas and glow-in-the-dark scorpions, to name a few. This is all done in a fun and kid friendly way (I of course had to cover my eyes).

Strollers are not allowed in the exhibit area, but can be parked in the inside at the great gift shop.

Butterfly Gardens
1461 Benvenuto, 250 652 3822
www.butterflygardens.com

You will be transported to the jungle...it is lush and it is humid, there are towering tropical plants, turtles, geckos, flamingos, oh, and butterflies! Download a butterfly reference chart before you go, and see if you can find all 75 spices of butterfly! While that may only appeal to older kids, the younger set will like wandering the windy path's and marveling at all the colorful birds and pretty butterflies!

Butterfly gardens is far from the main beat of downtown, situated on the Saanich Peninsula 5 minutes away from world famous Butchart Gardens, but around a 25 minute drive from the downtown core.

The paths throughout are stroller friendly.

Butchart Gardens
800 Benvenuto Avenue, 250 652 4422
http://www.butchartgardens.com/

While not every child's cup of tea, it can make for a nice afternoon. Butcharts is the Disneyland of gardens. There are many different areas to explore- all car free, and all stroller friendly.

Your kids can follow little paths that wind through beautiful gardens; there are ponds and bridges, and high peaks and low valleys. Most will want to take a turn on the old timey carousal.

Butcharts puts on a super charming Christmas light show in the month of December. In the summer there are evening fireworks (this happens at 10- so too late for most kids). Autumn you can see the maples change colours, and in spring all the flowers start to show.
I would give yourselves at least 2 hours to see everything at a casual pace!

There are a couple of different dining options and there are washrooms located throughout.

Shaw Ocean Discovery
9811 Seaport Place, Sidney, 250 665 7511
http://www.oceandiscovery.ca/
Adults $15, Children 7-17 $8, Children 3-6 $5, Under 3 Free
Dive deep in to the depths of the Discovery Center in an old copper submarine...you will be surprised at what is before your eyes when the hatch opens. Here you will find Victoria's only aquarium. Compared to other city's it is tiny. That said it is still worth a visit, especially if you plan to tour around Sidney anyway.

There are giant floor to ceiling tanks with all sorts of creatures found in the Salish Sea. If you are lucky the giant octopus will come out of hiding and reveal himself to you.

There are some learning experiences, and very nice and informative staff to help you along the way.

This activity will not take you long with really little ones, and even with older ones. The max amount of time I would give for this is 1 hour- but my son went through it in 6 minutes!

Horse and Buggy Tour
Belville and Menzies, http://www.tallyhotours.com or http://www.victoriacarriage.com/
Pricing depends on tour.
Another favorite of most children is a horse and buggy ride. There are a few companies that do this in Victoria-most operating from the corner of Belville and Menzies, on the edge of the Parliament Buildings. Though not particularly cheap, it does offer a nice relaxing way to see parts of Victoria and learn some interesting history-perfect for tired feet.

• FARMER'S MARKETS

Victoria is a very '100' mile city. We love and support our farmers here, thus there are many markets. For a full listing check out this web site, http://www.victoriaexplorer.com/do/list-of-farmers-markets/

A few of our favorites are:

Moss Street Market
http://www.mossstreetmarket.com/
Moss and Fairfield Rd at Sir James Douglas School
Saturday's 10-2 June- October
Tons of food, fresh gorgeous produce, live entertainment, and crafts. Try the mini donuts made with spelt flour, practically healthy, right?
There are also three great playgrounds, one is obvious (right at the Market), and the other two are behind the school.

Sidney Night Market
Thursday Evenings, Beacon Avenue, running May to late August
The whole main drag of Sidney is closed to traffic and vendors set up their wares. Fresh produce, food, crafts, and entertainment. It can be busy, but is worth the trek out there.

Oak Bay Night Market
Oak Bay Avenue between Wilmot Place and Monteray, Every 3rd Wednesday from 4-8 mid June to mid September
Again, the street is closed off so vendors can set up. Produce, baked goods, artists and more.

Victoria Public Market- Farmers Market
Wednesday's 11-3 at the Public Market in the Hudson
This market runs year round.

• SEASONAL GUIDE

Tourism Victoria has a great website:
**http://www.tourismvictoria.com/events/
calendar/**

Summer
Summer in Victoria is great. There are many events that happen annually, and most are in the downtown core. Here is a list of the more kid friendly ones. Check Tourism Victoria's website for actual dates & times.

June
TD International Jazz Festival
http://jazzvictoria.ca/jazz-fest
Various Venues, some free outdoor performances

Oak Bay Tea Party
http://www.oakbayteaparty.com/
This is like an old time fair. Rides, cotton candy, and games. This event is right at Willows Beach and is very kid friendly!

July
Buskers Festival
http://victoriabuskers.com/
Held at various street venues downtown, there are usually some pretty amazing sights to see. Picture two guys tossing around a chainsaw- or magicians pulling rabbits out of hats and you have the right idea.

August
Saanichton Fair
http://www.saanichfair.ca/

Another fair, lots of rides, games, and food. They also have 4H type of stuff, biggest squash contests, horse shows, and more. It can get pretty busy, but the kids always seem to have a blast.

Symphony Splash
http://victoriasymphony.ca/splash/
The Victoria Symphony sets up shop on a barge at the Inner Harbour and plays the most beautiful music. People set up blankets on the Parliament Building lawns and settle in for an evening of music.
The actual music starts around 7pm, so it may be too late for some little ones. There is a family zone from 1-4 that includes face painting and lots of musical hands on activities. This is usually on the lawns at the Parliament Buildings.

Fall
September
Rifflandia Music Festival
http://rifflandia.com/, **Royal Athletic Park**
This is the hippest of hip music festival's, so if music is your thing, check out the web site (past performers include Courtney Love, Death From Above 1979, Vince Vaccaro)- if the weather is nice, which it usually is, there is a ton of kid's stuff here, as well as some great food vendors, and of course the music!

Salmon Run
Goldstream National Park
http://www.goldstreampark.com/
Come watch the salmon struggle to make their way upstream to spawn. It is a neat way to teach kids about nature, but can be a little on the real side. Picture salmon carcasses being picked away at by greedy crows. If you don't mind that, then this is a fun place to go for a walk. There are some trails, and a nature house here.
The Salmon usually spawn from September through to October.

October
Galey Farm Pumpkin Patch and Train
http://www.galeyfarms.net/, 4150 Blenkinsop Road

This place can be a bit of zoo, but if you are up for it, it can be fun. There is a mini train, a petting zoo, bouncy castles, and of course the pumpkin patch.

Winter
December

There is a wack of Christmassy things to do in December. Check Tourism Victoria's website for detailed information:

Butchart Garden Festival of Lights
http://www.butchartgardens.com/

This is one of our favorite Christmas things to do. There are millions of twinkly little light displays and it is completely enchanting! They even have an outdoor skating rink (bring your own skates).

Laurel Point Inn Gingerbread House Display
http://laurelpoint.com/

Breeze through the hotel lobby and marvel at all the yummy and intricate gingerbread houses. You will need a treat after this one!

Empress Hotel Festival of Tree's
Empress Hotel

100's of decorated Christmas Tree's throughout the Empress Hotel, This is a fund raiser for BC Children's Hospital.

Santa Parade

Check Tourism Victoria's website for dates, times, and route.
Parade ends at City Hall where they light up the big tree.

Christmas Tree Light up in Oak Bay
http://www.visitoakbayvillage.ca/

A family fun event, the street is closed and there are all sorts of Christmas related activities- all ending with the store fronts turning on their Christmas lights.

Truck Light Parade

100's of trucks, cement mixers, and busses all dress up in Christmas lights and roll through the streets honking and blaring Christmas music. It's great fun.
Check out Tourism Victoria's website for date, time and route.

February
Chinese New Year Celebrations in China Town

Lots of fire crackers and dancing dragons. Chinese New Year is a fun and loud event! Check out Toursim Victoria's website for information.

Spring

While not many events happen in the spring, Victoria is beautiful! The spring blossoms and flowers are all coming up and the weather gets warmer.

Victoria Highland Games and Celtic Festival
http://www.visitoakbayvillage.ca/, Topaz Park

Get a taste of all things Scottish. Heavy lifting contests, bagpipe parades, concerts, dancing, and probably some haggis.

• THE SCENIC DRIVE

Kids fall asleep in the car? Need somewhere to drive to let them have at least a little bit of a nap? Or maybe you just want to take in some sights in the comfort of your car. Well then, great! Victoria has a very nice scenic drive. I would suggest starting at The Ogden Point Breakwater, but you could get on it at any point. You will drive East along Dallas Road and follow the clearly marked signs. This will take you along the cliffs, then wind through a little neighborhoody part in Fairfield, up along the high cliff's and stunning homes on King George Terrace, and then along Beach Drive in Oak Bay, through the Victoria Golf Course- then past Willows Beach, then on to Uplands Park and Cattle Point (a nice place to stop), and then through the old mansions of Uplands, ending up at Cadboro Bay Village.

It is a really nice drive with lots of nice things to see along the way. It takes around half an hour.

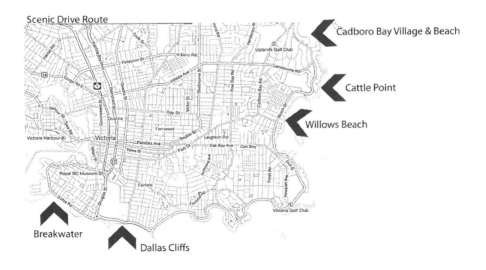

• VIC WEST

1. Banfield Park
   Spiral Cafe
   Fry's Bread
   Sailor Jacks
2. Selkirk Station
   (bike & Kayak rentals)
   Galloping Goose
3. Trestle
4. Spinnakers
5. Fol Epi
   Cafe Fantastico

Vic West is just on the other side of the 'Blue Bridge'. Accessible by foot, bus, harbour ferry, or car- it is worth a trip, especially if you are into food, as there are some amazing bakeries on this side of the bridge.

There are 3 main areas worth checking out- The Dockside Green, which is where you will find Fol Epi and Café Fantastico and part of the Galloping Goose trail. I recommend getting a sandwich and a coffee and then heading out on 'The Goose' for a little walk.

Then there is a one block section on Craigflower Rd, where there is a tiny shopping/eating strip directly across the street from Banfield Park. This is a great spot to grab a bite to eat, and then give the kids a good play!

Finally the West Songhee walkway, a continuation of the Galloping Goose Trail, and a really lovely seaside walk (and you can make the Spinnakers Brewpub your destination).

Sadly, Vic West is not really a shoppers paradise- but we won't hold that against it because it has so many other redeemable qualities.

If you need a grocery store there is a Save On Foods in the Westside Village. There is also a Liquor Store, Pharmacy, and a Walk In Health Clinic.

• EAT

Fol Epi
101-398 Harbour Rd, 250 477 8882
http://www.folepi.ca/
Right off of the Galloping Goose trail at Harbour Rd in the Dockside Green is Fol Epi, which is to die for. Using all organic ingredients, and grinding the flour on the premises, the bread is made in a wood burning oven and is everything you want bread to be, crusty on the outside, chewy on the inside with just a hit of sourness. It is perfection. They make amazing sandwiches, sometimes pizzas, always pastries, and in the summer ice cream.

Café Fantastico
102-398 Harbour Rd, 250 590 2315
http://caffefantastico.com/
Connected to Fol Epi is Café Fantastico, where you can get a good coffee.
There are just a few seats inside, but in warmer weather there is a big patio where you can sit and enjoy your goodies while the kids explore freely(ish).

Spinnakers
308 Catherine Street, 250 386 2379
http://www.spinnakers.com/

Located on the Songhee's walk way, this sit down gastro-brew pub has a great view and great food. They try to follow the 100 mile approach here, using local ingredients as much as possible. They also brew their own beer. They have a kid's menu, high chairs and are mostly stroller friendly (there are a couple of stairs).

Fry's Bread
416 Craigflower Rd, 250 590 5727
http://www.frysbakery.com/

Over on Craigflower Rd across the street from Banfield Park is Fry's Bread. They make the best croissant in Victoria- I swear! They also sell, among other things, sandwiches, breads, danish's, and cookies. They use only Red Fife Wheat Flour, a heritage grain which is native to Canada. On Sundays they make only pizzas, and stay open till they sell out. Everything is made from scratch on site- and is delicious!

Spiral Café
418 Craigflower Rd, 250 386 9303
Next door to Fry's is The Spiral Café, a funky and family friendly little coffee shop where you can get a nice coffee and a treat. They have a bin of toys at the back and don't mind the noise and mess of little children. Some Sunday's they have a story time, but it is inconsistent, so make sure you call before you go. Also, you won't find wifi here!

• SHOP

Sailor Jacks
424 Craigflower Rd, 250 382 5225
Sailor Jacks is a little children's consignment shop in the same strip as Fry's Bread and The Spiral Cafe. They have kids clothes, baby gear, and toys and a small selection of maternity wear.

• PLAY

Selkirk Station
106-80 Regatta Landing, 250 383 1466
http://selkirkstation.com/
There are a few places to rent bikes in Victoria; however, there are only a small handful of places to safely ride bikes with children in Victoria. I think if you are going to be adventurous and take the kids out, the Galloping Goose trail is a good car free place to do it. You can rent bikes, kid's bikes and trailers from Selkirk Station over in Vic West and then you will be directly on the Goose. They also rent Kayaks, which can be quite fun with older children (they have doubles, so your kids don't have to go it alone). Again, they are right on the Selkirk Waterway so it is easy and convenient and you can enjoy a nice paddle on the calm protected waters of The Gorge.

Galloping Goose
http://www.gallopinggoosetrail.com

The Galloping Goose is a huge trail system that winds it's way from downtown all the way out to Sooke. There is some stunning scenery along this long trail. The best way to see it is by bike...but if you have younger kids you can just take a walk on parts of it.

The part of The Goose that is in Vic West is perfect for this. It is stroller friendly. If you start in front of Fol Epi and head to the left (away from downtown) and walk for around 10 minutes you will end up at a fork, if you head to the left instead of going across the trestle you will find yourself on a path that takes you over to Banfield Park which has a great playground.

To the right at the fork will be an old trestle that spans the Selkirk Waterway. Kids love tearing across this bridge and seeing all the water activity below. Just be careful as there can be a lot of fast bicycle traffic on the bridge.

Once off of the trestle if you go to the right you can make your way along some more bridges, boardwalks, and walkways and you will find yourself in a neat little courtyard where the kids can run free.

Songhee's

The West Songhee Walkway is another stretch of the Goose. If you walk across the Johnson Street Bridge and stay left you will be on the walkway. It starts in front of the Delta Hotel (a perfect spot to use the washroom) and keeps on going for around 5 km into Esquimalt. There are a few little rocky beaches along this path that make a nice pit stop- perfect for throwing little stones into the ocean! Of course from here you can also spy sea planes, ferries, and the odd helicopter.

Spinnakers is around a 20 minute walk from the Delta Hotel and makes a nice destination for lunch.
You can also catch a little harbour ferry from downtown to a point on this path.

Banfield Park

Across the street from Fry's Bread, The Spiral Cafe and Sailor Jacks is this great playground. It is in the middle of a big field, one side is a giant hill that kids love rolling down and the other side the Gorge Waterway- which makes for an outstanding view.

There are tennis courts up-top, and The Goose path runs along the water here.

The playground is wood chipped, has swings, and two separate play structures- one suitable for older kids and the other for younger.

If you follow the path to the right you will end up at the trestle- this is a packed dirt path so it stroller friendly if you have a good stroller.

• OAK BAY

Oak Bay is a charming area. Considered one of Victoria's old money neighborhoods, Oak Bay is dotted with amazing big old houses. It is also a wonderful family neighborhood, with a nice selection of boutique shops and some good eats nestled throughout the small but cute shopping village. Most of it is contained to the 3 block strip between Elgin and Monterey. However there is also some must see places between Davie and Foul Bay. If you have time, and your kids have the patience you could walk the entire 9 or so blocks and see (and eat) everything. There are a couple of parks close by so you can run the children when you are finished and hopefully they will be happy!

If you need a grocery store there is a Fairway Market in the Village (as well as a liquor store). Across from that is a Pharmasave. There is also a Safeway with an in-store pharmacy (and another liquor store) at Fort and Foul Bay.

1. Abby Sprouts
2. Sceince Works
3. Red Fern Park
4. Discovery Coffee
5. Abra-kid-abra &
   The Whole Beast &
   The Village Butcher
6. Fawn
7. Finn & Izzy
   Ottavio
8. Windser Park

Ottavio
2272 Oak Bay Avenue (at Monterey), 250 592 4080 http://www.ottaviovictoria.com/

An inviting and delicious Italian Deli and Café at the far end of the Oak Bay strip, offering counter service... meaning it is pretty quick! The Café offers paninis, soups, salads, baked goods, gelato, Italian coffees, sodas, and even wine. Everything is made in house with quality ingredients. In the summer tables and chairs sprawl out into the front courtyard making it a nice place for lunch or a break with your kids.

On the deli side they have Italian dry goods, cheeses, salami and meats, olives, and more. It's a perfect place to grab some food for a meal later on.

Discovery Coffee
1964 Oak Bay Avenue (at Amphion Street) 250 590 7717, http://www.discoverycoffee.com/

Great little stop for a coffee and a treat. There is a hip vibe happening at the Oak Bay Discovery, with the warm wood interior and the vinyl records playing on the record player. Discovery roasts their own beans, and the baristas know their stuff. If you are lucky they won't be sold out of their decadent house made Yonni's Doughnuts.

The Whole Beast/Village Butcher
2032 Oak Bay Avenue, 250 590 7675 http://thewholebeast.com & 250 598 1115, http://villagebutcher.ca/

Housed together this is the place to get meat in Oak Bay. The Whole Beast offers up artisan cured meat, everything is house made, and uses local ethical ingredients wherever possible. Try the pepperoni- you won't be disappointed!

The Village Butcher is just that, a Butcher. They sell Island raised and ethically produced antibiotic free meats, as well as local eggs, and Fol Epi baguettes. On Saturdays they make killer sandwiches.

Starbucks
2182 Oak Bay Avenue, 250 598 8666
http://www.starbucks.ca/
Located in the heart of Oak Bay Avenue.

• SHOP

Abby Sprouts
1841 Oak Bay Avenue, 250 294 8978
http://www.abbysprouts.com/
Abby Sprouts is a great store that specializes in eco baby things. Clothes, diapers, toys, wraps, pregnancy and post postpartum items too. Its a few blocks up from the main drag, but worth popping in if you need anything.

Abra-kid-abra
2024 Oak Bay Ave, 250 595 1613
http://www.abra-kid-abra.com
Consignment and new items. A nice selection of toys and clothes, shoes, and gear- both new and used. They have a train table set up so your little ones can be amused while you shop! They also offer equipment rentals.

Timeless Toys
2213 Oak Bay Ave, 250 598 8697
http://www.timelesstoys.ca
Great toy store with a thoughtful selection of imaginative toys and games. They also have a train table set up in the back of the store.

Finn & Izzy
2259 Oak Bay Ave, 250 592 8168
http://www.finnandizzy.com
This is a great clothing/toy store. They have quality brands of clothing and accessories, a great selection of shoes, baby essentials, and amazing toys for kids of all ages. Their book section is especially wonderful.

Science Works
1889 Oak Bay Avenue, 250 595 6033
http://scienceworksvictoria.ca
A great store for your budding scientist with all sorts of neat things to look at. Lots of build it and experiment kits.

Fawn Children's Boutique
2225 Oak Bay Avenue, 250 590 5835
http://fawnkids.com
This is a super charming children's clothing boutique. They have brands you won't find anywhere else in the city. The store is bright and cheery, and there is a little play area to keep your babes busy while you shop.

• PLAY

Redfern Park
On Redfern between Leighton and Bouchier Street.
This a nice new construction park that is tucked away so it has a secluded feel. There is a big structure for older kids, and a smaller one for the little guys, as well as a swing set and a fairly big safe area for them to run around. Grab a coffee and a treat from Discovery Café on Oak Bay Avenue and walk 2 blocks to this park.
There is also a Safeway (and liquor store) within walking distance.

Windsor Park
Located on Windsor Street between Transit Street and Newport Avenue
There is a large field, washrooms, and a nice new playground. This park makes for a good destination at the end of an Oak Bay Avenue Stroll- grab some picnic things from Ottavio, and go for a play. The ocean is just two blocks from here, so you can always pop down to have a look at the sea.

Carnarvon Park
At Carnarvon & Henderson
This park/playground is not located near the Oak Bay strip- and is sort of in the middle of nowhere, however, it is a great park to make a special trip to in the summer. Carnarvon park is home to a pretty amazing water park. Pack a picnic and set up shop in the shade of one of the big tree's. There is plenty of splashing opportunities for the little ones here.

• ESTEVAN VILLAGE & WILLOW'S BEACH

Willow's Beach and the Estevan Village is still considered Oak Bay, but this is special area, so it gets its own write up. A nice way to spend the day is to hit up Willow's Beach for a stroll and a play, and then either walk or drive up to Estevan Village. In Estevan Village you will find Victoria's only Cafe that has an attached play area for the kids. The food is great here, and the kids will surely be amused. There are also a few shops to poke around in. This area really has it all!

If you need a grocery store there is a little one across from Pure Vanilla on Cadboro Bay Road.

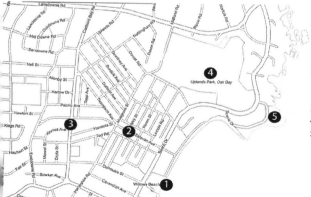

1. Willows Beach
2. Crumsby's Cupcake Cafe
   The Village Cafe
   Buddies Toys
3. Pure Vanilla
4. Uplands Park
5. Cattle Point

Crumsby's Cupcake Café
2509 Estevan Avenue, 250 595 2221
http://crumsbys.com/

Offering counter service, highchairs, a great changing area, wooden toys galore, this is Victoria's only Kindercafe (café/playroom). In this cheerful clean room you can have delicious food, all made from scratch with care, and your children can play with some pretty cool toys. They have yummy coffee and baked goods too! It can get a bit hectic in here on weekends and rainy days, but the kids never seem to mind.

The Village Café
2518 Estevan Avenue, 250 592 8311
http://thevillagerestaurant.ca/
If you crave something a little less crazy head across the street to The Village Café. Simple but tasty fair, in a less kid centric setting. They have highchairs, but no baby change table. They serve breakfast all day (among other things).

Pure Vanilla
2590 Cadboro Bay Road, 250 592 2596
Up on Cadboro Bay Road this place is great (but busy). They have mouth watering treats, healthy soups, salads, pizzas, good coffee, and more. There are tables and chairs in a little courtyard in the back where watched kids can wander around.

• SHOP

Buddies Toy's
2533 Estevan Ave, 250 595 6501
http://buddiestoys.ca
Another one of Victoria's great toy stores. Chockablock full of eco and imagination based toys with a train table to amuse the kiddies while you shop. They also have a big selection of games and very helpful staff.

• PLAY

Uplands Park
The main entrances into Uplands Park are located on Beach Drive, Dorset Road, and Midland Road.
Uplands Park offers numerous walking trails. The park is a pretty vast wild stretch of undeveloped land, complete with little bluffs, open fields, and paths throughout a light forest. It is a great place to picnic in the summer and really let the kids explore nature. In the winter and colder months it's still fun to bundle up and trek through here. Especially if you can warm up with a hot chocolate at Crumsby's after!

Cattle Point

Cattle point is considered part of Uplands Park and runs along Beach Drive. This is also a fun area to explore... you can bramble along the rocks along the ocean's edge as you watch kayakers go by.

Willows Beach

Willows is a fantastic beach. There is a playground just beyond the parking lot, complete with swings and two different sized play areas. And then there is the beach... it is a long stretch of white sand that extends a good bit in both directions, perfect for gathering little treasures, or even swimming in the summer.

There is a concession here- it is pretty 'concessiony', so if you can hold out for better food I would recommend that (or come with a picnic). There are washrooms right at the playground.

• CADBORO BAY

Carry along past Willow's Beach, around 10 minutes by car, and you will come to Cadboro Bay Village. The highlight of this area is Gyro Park and Cadboro Bay Beach. There is a little grocery store and a cafe, so you can get coffees and snacks to either enjoy in the Village or bring to the beach.

1. Olive Olio's
   Peppers Foods
   Starbucks
2. Gyro Park
   Cadboro Bay Beach

• EAT

Olive Olio's
3840 Cadboro Bay Road, 250 477 6618
Counter service, right in the heart of the Cadboro Bay Village. It's an ok place with kid friendly fair, sandwiches and that sort of thing. In the winter there is not a lot of room in here for strollers, and there are no highchairs. In the summer there are seats outside, which is kind-of nice.

Peppers Foods
3829 Cadboro Bay Road, 250 477 6513
http://peppers-foods.com/
Peppers Foods is a grocery store with a great selection of products.   It is really easy to rustle up the makings for a wonderful picnic here.

Starbucks
3849 Cadboro Bay Road, 250 382 8119
http://www.starbucks.ca/

• PLAY

Gyro Park/Cadboro Bay
Here you find a pretty amazing playground, complete with giant climbable octopus and sea monster sculptures. There is also a cool old ship that kids can climb around that is sure to amuse.   Right beyond the playground is the bay.   This is a nice stretch of beach- the water is very shallow for a long way out, so it is great for toddlers to splash safely around in.   It's fun to watch the skim boarders at the far end of the beach.

• FERNWOOD

Fernwood is less than a 10 minute drive from downtown. Mainly a residential area, with some nice old Victorian homes, there are a few notable things that kids may enjoy (and so might you). The hub of this area is at Gladstone and Fernwood where you will find some eats, a coffee shop, and The Belfry Theater. There is a little playground at the Fernwood Community Center just down Gladstone (towards downtown). There is also a Drop-in Kindergym at the Fernwood Community Center. The cost is $2. However, if you have limited time in Victoria I would skip this area.

There is a small specialty foods market on Gladstone (Aubergine). Or you can try Wellburns on Pandora and Cook.

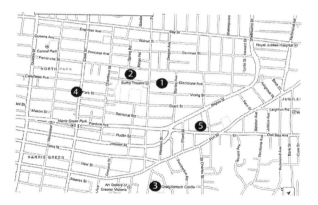

1. Cornerstone Cafe
2. Fernwood Community Center
3. Craigdarroch Castle
4. Mount Royal Bagels
   Parsonage Cafe
5. Stadaconna Park
   Origin Bakery

• EAT

Fernwood Inn
1302 Gladstone Avenue, 250 412 2001
http://www.fernwoodinn.com/

A friendly pub like setting where your kids will feel at home. Casual fair and a casual atmosphere...the burgers are great- and it's not too fussy.

Cornerstone Coffee Shop
1301 Gladstone Avenue, 250 381 1884

On the corner of Fernwood and Gladstone in an old brick building streaming with light is the Cornerstone Coffee Shop. It has great coffee and baked goods. They have live music Wednesday and Friday nights.

Mount Royal Bagel Factory
6-1115 North Park Street, 250 380 3588

Closer to downtown just off of Cook Street their door is actually on Caledonia Street, and they make the best bagel in Victoria. The real deal, Montreal style bagels, boiled, so they are nice and chewy. They offer bagels and cream cheese to-go- as it is not a sit down kind of place.

Parsonage Cafe
1115 North Park Street, 250 383 5999

Around the corner from Mount Royal is The Parsonage Cafe. It has undergone some changes lately and is now a no frills hip counter service coffee shop and eatery. They serve lighter fare, sandwiches, soups, salads, baked goods...and the menu is built around seasonal availability using as much locally sourced ingredients as possible.

Origins Bakery
1525 Pandora Avenue, 250 590 4149
http://www.originbakery.com/

Located across the street from Stadacona Park, Origin's Bakery is the best place in Victoria to get gluten free breads and baked goods. The éclairs are truly amazing!

• PLAY

Fernwood Community Center (Playground and Drop In Kindergym)
1240 Gladstone Avenue, 250 381 1552
http://fernwoodnrg.ca/neighbourhood/
fernwood-community-centre/
Head down Gladstone Avenue towards town and you will see the community center. To get to the playground go down the stairs on your right, and you will see it up on the hill. This is a decent playground for your kids to run off some steam. It has that weird rubber 'flooring', so if they have a big fall, it likely won't hurt as much!

There is also a Drop-in Kindergym at the Fernwood Community Center, which is good for a rainy day (or not). It is held in the gym which gives kids plenty of room to run around and act crazy!

Stadacona Park
Located on Pandora Ave between Elford Street and Belmont Ave.
There is a nice sized playground, a big manicured garden area, tennis courts, washrooms, picnic tables and benches as well as a nice hill for rolling down.
It is conveniently across from Origin's Gluten Free Bakery

• FAIRFIELD

Fairfield is a cool neighborhood with lots going for it. The majority of it is residential with a lot of families and students. There are a couple of main areas to check out in Fairfield. There is the Cook Street Village, which has some great restaurants, and a couple of shops and then there is a small pocket near Gonzales Beach. It's main draw however, is Beacon Hill Park and Dallas Road. Beacon Hill Park is the home to two great playgrounds, a water park, a petting zoo, a putting green, beautiful gardens, ducks, ponds, and more. Dallas Road has a scenic walkway that runs from the Ogden Point breakwater to Clover Point and offers amazing views of the Straight as well as plenty of good people and dog watching! Part of the walkway is directly across from Beacon Hill Park. You can also make your way down below to the rocky beach below and comb along it listening to the waves crash and searching for beach glass and other treasures.

If you need to get a little grocery shopping done there are a few choices. There is the Fairfield Plaza at Fairfield Road and Street Charles across from Ross Bay Cemetery. There is a Thrifty Foods, Peoples Drug Mart, and a liquor store here. Or if you are in the Cook Street Village area there is Mothers Market- which has a great selection of natural and organic foods. There is also a good cold beer and wine store in the parking lot behind the pharmasave.

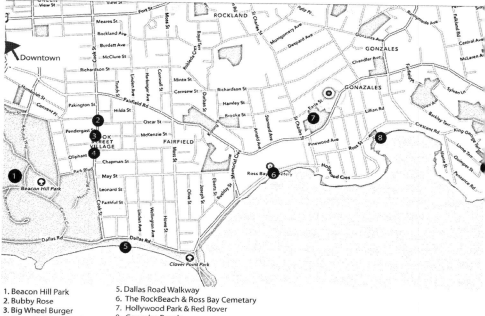

1. Beacon Hill Park
2. Bubby Rose
3. Big Wheel Burger
4. Pizzaria Prima Strada
   & Mother Natures
   & Rainbird Botique

5. Dallas Road Walkway
6. The RockBeach & Ross Bay Cemetary
7. Hollywood Park & Red Rover
8. Gonzales Beach
9. Quimper Park

• EAT

Bubby's Kitchen
355 Cook Street (at Oscar), 250 590 8915
http://www.bubbyskitchen.ca/

This is home of Victoria's best chocolate chip cookie (possibly even Worlds best). Try it, you will not be sorry! Bubby's is split into two different sides, a café with table service (and a great patio in the summer), and a counter service deli side.

The food here is good made from scratch home-style cooking. Lots of options for vegetarians, vegans, and people on a gluten free diet.

The take out side has sandwiches, pizzas, baked goods, healthy salads, and such.

It is a little tight in here, but they do have high chairs, a kid's menu, and a baby change table.

Big Wheel Burger
341 Cook Street, 250 381 0050
http://bigwheelburger.com/

Big Wheel Burger is a pretty special burger place. Modeled after Shake Shack in the States, Big Wheel serves no nonsense fast food burgers made with ethically sourced and antibiotic free beef. The menu is simple and tasty. They have a kid's menu, high chairs, gluten free choices, and are carbon neutral to boot.

Starbucks
320 Cook Street, 250 380 7606
http://www.starbucks.ca/

Pizzeria Prima Strada
230 Cook Street, 250 590 8595
http://www.pizzeriaprimastrada.com/
Traditional Wood Fire Thin Crust Pizza at it's best. This is true Neapolitan pizza, which when done perfectly, as it is here, is crispy, tender, and fragrant. They use traditional Italian practices and ingredients, as well as sourcing things locally. Kids love it here, there is a big woodfire oven where they can watch the chefs working the pizzas, tossing the dough high into the air. It's busy, noisy, and the food is really tasty. They have high chairs and coloring stuff for the kids.
We will often get our pizzas to go, and take them over to Beacon Hill Park for a little picnic.

Mothers Nature's Market and Deli
240 Cook Street, 250 590 7390
http://www.mothernaturesbc.ca/
Mother's is a great natural grocery store. They have a great grocery selection, as well as health foods, beauty things, and a deli. The deli is a good place to grab picnic goodies to take over to Beacon Hill Park.

• SHOP

Rainbird
**101-240 Cook Street, 250 381-3767 http://www.
rainbirdboutique.com/**
A cute little shop in the Cook Street Village that sells stylish and fun raingear for adults and children, think Hunter and Hatley.

Red Rover
1722 Lillian Rd, 250 440 6353
**https://www.facebook.com/pages/Red-Rover-
Kids-Consignment**
A darling consignment store across from Hollywood Park that has a well chosen selection of clothes and toys and great prices!

Beacon Hill Park
http://www.beaconhillpark.ca/

Beacon Hill Park is Victoria's Central Park. It is spread across 200 acres and lies just beyond downtown. It has well manicured garden areas connected by little paths and bridges. There are duck ponds, a petting zoo, two playgrounds, a putting green, and more. In the summer there is a band stand where musicians play.

It runs along Douglas Street between Southgate and Dallas Rd, and it starts on Cook Street just beyond the Cook Street Village at May Street.

Playgrounds

The 'New Playground,' as the locals call it, is at Cook and May. This is a pretty amazing playground and is always bustling. There is a zip-line, a big net climby thing, swings, a big and little play structure, and sand area with a big dinosaur to climb on. It is surrounded by a big green lawn and there are plenty of benches for parents to sit and chat. You can also find washrooms here.

The other playground is in the middle of the park just beyond the washrooms. There are structures for both bigger and little kids, swings- and in the summer there is a small cemented water park that is great fun.

Petting Zoo

The petting zoo is by donation and located on Circle Dr (across from the putting green), with plenty of parking. Here you can check out all sorts of fowl (there are some really crazy looking punk rock chickens), pigs, llamas, miniature horses, bunnies, and more. Of course the highlight is petting the goats and watching them frolic around.

If you show up at 10:10 you can witness the legendary Running of the Goats- which is when the goats are moved from their overnight home to the day time pen. People line up on each side of the path and clap as the goats go by. It's pretty hysterical!

Across from the Petting Zoo is a putting green. Unfortunately there are no rentals here- so you have to bring your own putters. If you can get your hands on them, this is great fun.

Hollywood Park
On Fairfield Road between St.Charles and Earle Street.

Hollywood park is on Fairfield Rd. In the summer you can get a hotdog from the concession and take in a minors baseball game. There is a playground and tennis courts here too. This park within is walking distance to Red Rover- so ideally you would start at Red Rover, do a quick shop, head over to the Fairfield Plaza and get a Starbucks, then a sandwich from the Thrify Foods deli, and walk over to the park for a little play.

Dallas Road Walkway
On Dallas Road between Clover Point and the Ogden Point Breakwater

Edging along the ocean is Dallas Rd, part of Victoria's scenic drive route, it also offers a great place to walk along the cliffs. There are always people out for a stroll here, so the people and dog watching is great.

Clover Point is a great place to fly a kite, and further down the walkway there are often people kite boarding, which is pretty swell to watch.

A little closer to the breakwater on the walkway is a little pond. Most days there are people maneuvering remote control boats around the water.

There are many paths that lead down from the walkway to various beaches along Dallas Rd. Kids love brambling along the shoreline, finding hidden treasures.

The Rock Beach/ Cemetery
On Dallas Road between Memorial Crescent and Street Charles Street
Further along Dallas Rd (east) just past clover point is a beach we call the rock beach. It is right across from beautiful Ross Bay Cemetery.

This beautiful beach is covered in little perfect smooth round pebbles, and the water is crystal clear. This is not a swimming or wading beach as the water drops off very deep right away...but it is a nice beach for little ones to poke around and gather rocks and sea glass and such.

We like to come here and throw rocks into the ocean and see if we can spot otters making their way across the bay.

If you cross the road you can walk through the cemetery, which is pretty stunning. Most of the gravestones date back to the 1800's. Keep your eye out for the resident deer!

There are some basic no frill's washrooms at the corner of Dallas and Memorial Crescent in the cemetery.

Gonzales Beach
At Ross Street and Roberson Street
Keep driving down Dallas Rd to the east and it will turn
into Hollywood Crescent...Take a right when you get
to Ross Street and park. Now you will be at Gonzales
Beach. There are washrooms at the top. Walk down the
hill from here towards the ocean you will find a stretch
of sandy beach. In the winter and fall this is a favorite
dog beach, so be prepared for that- if you like dogs it's
great!

In the summer people come here to spend the day. The
water is fairly shallow for a ways out, good for splashing
around...keep in mind that the ocean here never gets
that warm.

Quimper Park
Quimper Street between Crescent Rd and Maquinna Street

This is Victoria's 'toy' park. I am assuming that the neighborhood people have been dropping off toys at this park for years...so there is a great assortment of trucks, kitchens, sand toys, sometimes ride-em's...all sorts of things in addition to the usual swings and monkey bars and slides.

There is no coffee shop down here, so bring in your own eats and treats.

Quimper Park is located on a little point, so if you and the kids are up for a small walk you can do a little loop and see a few neat things along the way. Head left out of the park, turn right on Crescent Road, if you walk down towards the water you can see the Chinese Cemetery and a little tiny beach. Walk along the cemetery's perimeter and follow the road to the right and you will find a little path, follow that path up Maquinna Street, then take the first right and you will be back at the park.

• JAMES BAY

James Bay is one of Victoria's oldest neighborhoods and a short distance from downtown. Very residential, it is a hodgepodge of 80's apartment buildings and character houses. The main draw is the Fisherman's Wharf area- where you will find a great park and playground and lots to see and do.

If you need supplies there is a Thrifty Foods, Pharmasave, and liquor store at the intersection of Menzies and Simcoe (just up from Discovery Coffee).

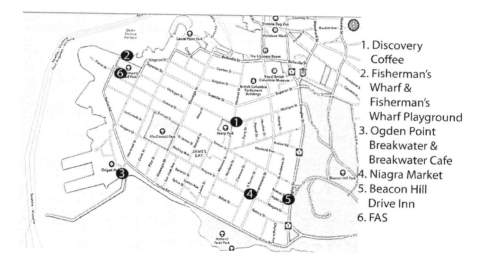

1. Discovery Coffee
2. Fisherman's Wharf & Fisherman's Wharf Playground
3. Ogden Point Breakwater & Breakwater Cafe
4. Niagra Market
5. Beacon Hill Drive Inn
6. FAS

• EAT

Discovery Coffee
281 Menzies Street, 250 590 6323
http://www.discoverycoffee.com/
There is another location of Victoria's own Discovery Coffee. The shop is not located near Fisherman's Wharf- but if you are inclined, visit it. They roast their own beans and thus have great coffee, really tasty treats, and a cool vibe going on.

There is a little park across the street from Discovery, however sometimes you have to share it with some harmless, but rough looking homeless people.

Finest At Sea (FAS)
27 Erie Street, 250 383 7760
http://www.finestatsea.com/
Located on Erie Street, just across from the Fisherman's Wharf Playground is a seafood retail outlet of FAS, whose main gig is wholesaling to many of Victoria's top restaurants. They have a little food truck that is parked in front of their retail store where you can get some outstanding fish and chips, as well as cold smoked tuna taco's and amazing chowder. We usually send a member of our party over to order and wait for the food while we have a play in the playground- and then we spread out with a little picnic and enjoy.

Fisherman's Wharf
Edged by Erie and Street Lawrence Street
http://fishermanswharfvictoria.com/
If you feel like lunch on the dock, there are some good choices. Barb's Fish and Chips is a Victoria Institution. Puerto Vallarta Amigos offers authentic Mexican Food. And if you want ice cream, Jackson's is the place to go.

Breakwater Café & Bistro
199 Dallas Rd, 250 386 8080
http://www.breakwaterbistro.ca/

Right at the entrance to The Breakwater is this busy little café. They have light fare, are stroller friendly, and quick counter service. If you need to use washroom after a walk on The Breakwater, they don't seem to notice if you don't buy anything.

Beacon Drive In
126 Douglas Street, 250 385 7521
http://www.beacondrivein.ca/

This Victoria institution has been serving up soft serve ice cream treats for over 50 years. This is the place to come and get a cone either before or after a trip to Beacon Hill Park. In the summer time the line can be long, but they move through it pretty quick. They offer food as well, think burgers, chicken strips, fries, and other deep fried options.

In the colder months they have a heated and covered outdoor patio, as well as a few booths inside.

Niagara Market
579 Niagara Street, 250 383 1223
http://getfreshwithalocal.com/

This tiny market on Niagara Street in James Bay is great market with a whole lot of heart. They carry a ton of local produce, local baked goods, organics, cheeses, local salamis and more. They also have an espresso machine, so you can get a coffee to go with your pastry.

• PLAY

Fisherman's Wharf
http://fishermanswharfvictoria.com/

This is a great place to go in James Bay. Fisherman's Wharf boasts a whole lot of family fun. You can check out it's collection of funky float homes, eat, often listen to live music, feed the seals, walk up to the playground at the top of the hill, as well as take in other harbour sites such as float planes, ferries, whale watching boats and such.

There is plenty of pay parking in the area, or if you drive around there is limited free street parking.

You can also access Fisherman's Wharf via the walkway from downtown. The walkway is a nice way to do it if your kids have the stamina. It takes around 20 minutes and is stroller friendly.

Or, you can catch one of the little water taxi's from downtown.

There are whale watching tours that leave from Fisherman's Wharf as well as the Pirate Adventures.

Feeding the Seals

To the left of Puerto Vallarta Amigo's you will usually see a small crowd gathered feeding the seals. You can either just watch, or you can buy fish to feed them at the fish stand directly behind.

Pirate Adventure
250 858 7535, Fisherman's Wharf
http://www.pirateadventures.ca/Victoria/

Victoria Pirate Adventures runs from May to mid September. This is a great thing to do with slightly older children- I would say 5 and above. It does take around 2 hours, and you will be on a boat, so make sure your kids have that sort of stamina and attention span!

First they dress you up in old timey pirate garb, then they take you on an adventure thought the harbour. These guys work very hard and put on a great show! So if you have a pirate buff on your hands, do it! Remember to pack an extra layer of clothes though, as it can get cold out at sea!

Fisherman's Wharf Park
On Erie Street between Street Laurence Street and Dallas Road
This Park is situated on the hill behind Fisherman's Wharf. It is built for bigger kids, but my little ones seem to enjoy it all the same. There are no swings, but there is a big slide, a bouncy car, and some climbing stuff. It has wood chips and a great view. The playground sits in a big huge grassy field. There are gentle hills, perfect for rolling down. There are wooden bridges and walkways over a demonstrational garden that little ones like to explore...there is even a tiny sandy beach area for digging.

Ogden Point Breakwater
Accessible on Dallas Road between Montreal and Dock Streets

The Ogden Point Breakwater is a nice place to spend an hour or so. It is further along Dallas Road- a ten minute walk from Fisherman's Wharf. There is plenty of street parking for free.

There is a walkway on the top of the breakwater that is suitable for strollers. Recently a guard rail has been put up, which makes it feel much safer for young walkers.

From the breakwater you can see all sorts of sea activity; sea planes, boats, fishermen, and sometimes sea life. If you are without a stroller and with older children then it's fun to walk along the lower levels, which is made up of huge slabs of stone. There is no guardrail here, so I would not recommend it for little children as it is uneven and sometimes wet. Older children will love hopping from slab to slab (sometimes the gaps between can be a few inches apart). This is where you will see people fishing and really get to see, smell, and hear the ocean.

There is a small sandy beach at the entrance to the breakwater that is perfect for beachcombing.

You can also stop at the Breakwater Cafe for a little bite or to warm up on cold days.

• DOWNTOWN

Downtown Victoria is pretty charming. Buildings with old world charm, unique shopping, and easy walkabilty make it a good place to be.

While there are not any playgrounds right in the core, there are a few places where kids can run off some steam.

Both Bastion Square and Market Square are car free areas where you can go with a coffee and your kids can bump around. Market Square is a little better for this as the lower part is contained, and it's hard (not impossible) for your kids to escape. The Atrium building at the corner of Blanshard and Yates has an indoor area where you can get a coffee and your kids can do some exploring. Note, these are not official play areas, just places with a little extra space...

There is also the Inner Harbour where you can wander and check out the artists selling there wares. This area is touristy though, as long as you are prepared for this fun can still be had.

Government Street, the main tourist drag, has some shops, like Seeing Is Believing, that kids are bound to like.

Johnson Street between Wharf and Government has great boutique shopping, especially for the mamas. Hip Baby is located here, as well as Market Square.

If you need to get groceries your best bet is The Market on Yates, which is in the Harris Green Shopping Plaza. There is a London Drugs, Walk-in Clinic and a Cold Beer and Wine store here to. If you find yourself down on Store Street there is a little health food store (Ingredients Health and Food Store) at Store and Discovery.

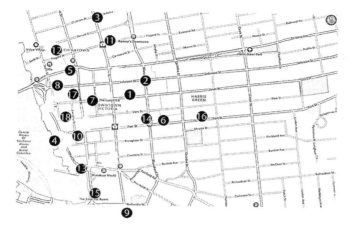

1. Hernandez
2. The Atrium Building
   Pig BBQ, Habit, Zambri's
3. White Spot
4. Red Fish Blue Fish
5. Habit
6. Choux Choux
   Chorizo & Co
7. Azuma Sushi
8. Market Square
   Hip Baby, Oscar & Libby's
   Mexi-Go Cafe, Wanna Waffle
   Zydeco, Willies Bakery
9. Old Spaghetti Factory
10. Bastion Square
    Paradiso Di Stelle
11. Hudson Market

12. Chinatown
13. The Causeway
    Milestones
14. Baan Thai
15. The Empress Hotel
16. Mothering Touch
17. Kaboodles
18. Nest & Cradle

• EAT

Hernandez
735 Yates Street, 250 884 5313
http://www.hernandezcocina.com/

Located in a small mall off of Yates between Douglas and Blanshard Street, Hernandez is easy to miss, but it should not be. This place has fantastic Mexican style food for cheap. Everything is made from scratch on the premises. Kids will enjoy the relaxed atmosphere and the usually fast paced arrival of your food. Tables covered in cheery oil cloth are set up in an indoor courtyard of the walk-through area of a small mall, so it is ok if your kids do not sit down for the entire meal. The tacos are amazing, as are the power-bars.
They have high chairs and are stroller friendly.
Bring cash if you go, as it is all they will accept.

Pig BBQ Joint
1325 Blanshard Street, 250 590 5193
http://pigbbqjoint.com/

Pig is a Victoria staple. It started out literally in a hole in the wall, but recently moved to the concrete, steel, and glass Atrium Building. You will get counter service at Pig, so you can get in and out of there quickly. Prices are very reasonable, and the food, classic southern bbq (fried chicken, pulled pork poutine, brisket sandwiches) is sinful and delicious. They have highchairs and are stroller friendly (but no kid's menu downtown).

White Spot
710 Caledonia Avenue, 250 382 9911
https://www.whitespot.ca/
While I usually lean towards recommending independent restaurants, White Spot is an exception. Mainly because you can get sit down service with a smile, and your kids can be comfortable being kids. Meaning it is not stuffy or fancy. They are known for their burgers, but have a wide variety of other items. They have a kids menu, colouring stuff, and high chairs, and an area in the front where you can park your stroller.

Red Fish Blue Fish
1006 Wharf Street, 250 298 6877
http://www.redfish-bluefish.com/
Located down on the Wharf in an up-cycled cargo container, Red Fish Blue Fish is a great place to get some seafood. Everything is fresh as can be, and completely sustainable. Be warned however all seating is outdoors, and the line up can be very long. Once you get your order in though, the food comes quickly. If you have help, ie someone to wait in line, this can be a fun place for kids, as they can check out ships and float planes coming and going and maybe even see the famous blue bridge go up.

The food here is excellent. Try the Tacone's or the Fish 'n' Chips.

No high chairs, but completely stroller friendly as it is outside.

Check their website before you go, as they are closed in the cold winter months.

Habit
**808 Yates Street (The Atrium), 250 590 5953
or 552 Pandora Avenue, 250 294 1127
http://habitcoffee.com/**
Habit is the hippest hipster coffee shop in town. There are two locations, the original is on Pandora just down from Government Street, and the new location is in the Atrium Building at Yates and Blanshard.
Great coffee, decent baked goods, and usually a little cool hipster attitude. If you don't mind the attitude, both are roomy, so you can spread out with all your stuff and relax and watch the people come and go.
They don't have highchairs, but are stroller friendly.

Zambri's
820 Yates Street, 250 360 1171 http://www.zambris.ca/
Also located in the Atrium, Zambri's makes some of the best Italian food Victoria has to offer. This is real Italian though, not Americanized as most people are used to. The food here is simple, flavorful and real. They lean towards seasonal eating, and use as many local suppliers as possible. The staff is well trained and knowledgeable.
While it can get a bit hoity-toity later in the evenings, it is perfectly acceptable to go with your kids for lunch or for an earlier dinner seating. Try to get a seat in the atrium patio, and then your kids can wander a bit while you keep on eye on them from your seat.
They will make a simple pasta or pizza for your children, and they have high chairs.

Choux Choux
**830 Fort Street, 250 382 7572
http://chouxchouxcharc.com/**
Located on Fort Street just up from Blanshard, Choux Choux is an amazing if not crammed deli, specializing in charcuterie (cured meats), pates, and cheeses. They have a daily special and soup and usually two different types of sandwiches. There are only a couple of seats, and because of this do a steady to-go business. So if you are looking for a quick lunch and are in the area, do stop in.

Chorizo and Co
807 Fort Street, 250 590 6393

Across the street from Choux Choux is Chorizo and Co, another great place to get a quick bite. They offer sandwiches, and a few other items, all tasty. They have a few more tables then Choux Choux, so if you can manage to get one, you can enjoy your lunch inside. They don't have high chairs, but you can usually squish a stroller in.

Azuma Sushi
615 Yates Street, 250 382 8768
http://www.azuma.ca/

On the corner of Government and Broad Street, Azuma is a large sushi place. It is sit-down service, and usually quite quick despite being so busy. They are tolerant of kids and have high chairs.

Romeo's
1703 Blanshard Street, 250 383 2121
http://www.romeos.ca/

Romeo's has been around for over 30 years. This is not your thin slice artisan Italian pizza, this is your crusty doughy ooey gooey cheesy pizza. Located on Blanshard and Fisgard, this is a big space, so getting a table is usually not a problem. This is a good place to bring kids, as the food is usually what kids like. Carbs! It is fast paced and loud in here, so your loud kids won't be a spectacle.

They have highchairs and can accommodate strollers.

Cafe Mexi-Go
1425 Store Street, 250 386 1425
http://cafemexigo.com/

On the Store Street side of Market Square you can pop in to this little Mexican Café and grab a quick bite. The food is fresh and made to order. There are high chairs and they can make something simple for your children.

Willie's Bakery
537 Johnson Street, 250 381 8414
http://williesbakery.com/

On lower Johnson Street this Café/bakery serves it up good. The food is tasty and the service quick. They have a sit-down area with table service, as well as a pastry case with goodies to go. It is a crowded place, so it can be a little annoying if you are laden with a big stroller.

The Old Spaghetti Factory
703 Douglas Street, 250 381 8445
http://www.oldspaghettifactory.ca/

This is Americanized Italian food in its purest. Not a foodies haven by any stretch, but it seems to work for kids, and for when you feel like just not caring what people think.

If you forgot to pack a lunch and are panic hungry, The Old Spaghetti Factory is located one block from the museum.

They have plenty of high chairs and an uber affordable kid's menu.

Wanna Waffle
102-560 Johnson Street, 250 590 5300
http://www.wannawafel.com/

Tucked in the corner of the Johnson Street entrance to Market Square is Wanna Waffle. The smell wafting from this tiny shop will certainly draw you in to try these authentic Belgium waffles. They have counter service, and are stroller friendly.

Paradiso Di Stelle
10 Bastion Square, 250 920 7266

If you are going to go check out Bastion Square and are looking for a coffee or light snack, this is the place to go. They have a nice little patio which is open in the summer months and perfect for people watching. This is a counter service place, so expect it to be quick!

Victoria Public Market at the Hudson
1701 Douglas Street, 250 884 8552
http://victoriapublicmarket.com/
Hudson's Market is new to the Victoria Food Scene and is located in the old Hudson's Bay Building on Fisgard and Douglas Street.

There a few fantastic choices here as far as food goes. Indian, Mexican, roasted meat sandwiches (the best meatball sub I have ever had is right here at Roast), pies, as well as some more deli/grocery type shops; Salt Spring Island Cheese, Island Spice Trade, Island Seafood, a bakery, and soon to come a grocery store. And don't forget about 2% Jazz on the Fisgard side. They roast their own coffee beans in house
.

They are all housed in a big modern wood, concrete, and steel hall with tables here and there. It is a perfect place to bring kids as the casual setting affords them some freedom, and you are sure to find something that appeals to everyone's tastes.

If you enter off on the Douglas side it is manageable with a stroller.

There is also a farmers market every Wednesday 11-3

Milestones
812 Wharf Street, 250 381 2244
http://www.milestonesrestaurants.com/
Perched above the Inner Harbor Milestones is another chain restaurant- however they do deliver in taste and service. The food is above average, the menu holds something for everyone, and they have kid's items, as well as high chairs. If you are lucky to get a seat at the window, your kids will be mesmerized with the harbor activity.
They have highchairs, a place to stow your stroller, as well as a kid's menu.

Baan Thai
1117 Blanshard Street, 250 383 0050
http://baanthaivictoria.ca/
This is a little hole in the wall Thai restaurant on Blanshard Street, between View and Fort. The locals love it here and it is always busy. If you like Thai food, this is the place to go. The service is good, it is bustling (so loud kids won't be noticed), and the food comes out quickly. It can be a bit tight with a stroller, but usually it can be made to work, and they do have highchairs.

• SHOP

Hip Baby
560 Johnson, 250 385 8020 http://www.hipbaby.com/
Located on the Johnson Street side of Market Square Hip Baby is a delightful store- they specialize in hip modern and cool eco toys, clothing, and baby items as well as a interesting selection of books and décor. They also have a mother's area where you can change a diaper or nurse a baby.

Mothering Touch
975 Fort Street, 250 595 4905
http:// www.motheringtouch.ca
Located on Fort Street between Quadra and Vancouver, Mothering Touch has a great selection of toys, feeding stuff, clothing, books and baby gear for newborns and smaller children. They also offer some playgroups, and other drop in classes like mom and me yoga.

Scallywags
624 Fort Street, 250 360 2570
http://www.scallywags-island.ca
Located on the Fort Street side of The Bay Center Scallywag's is predominantly a children's clothing store. They also sell well made shoes, and do have a good selection of thoughtful toys as well. The best thing is the train table and kitchen in the back, so the kids can play while you shop.

Kaboodle's Toys
1320 Government Street, 250 383 0931
http://www.kaboodlestoystore.com/locations/
victoria-toy-store/
Located on Government between Johnson and Yates, Kaboodles is a great toy store! They have a fabulous selection and helpful staff that will ensure you do n't leave empty handed.

Seeing is Believing
1020 Government Street
http://www.seeingisbelievinggifts.com/
This is a fun chain, there is a location on Government Street as well as in Mayfair mall. Older kids will have a ball in here, there is a lot to see and get hands on with. Boardgames, puzzles, crafts, and magic... with items ranging from educational to the newest gadgets, to gag gifts. You can find anything here for ages 0 to 200.

Zydeco
565 Johnson Street, 250 389 1877
www.zydecogifts.com
Another gag gift store with a bit of a nostalgic twist... think rubber duckies, Gumby and Pokey, lots to look at. Older kids will get a kick out of it for sure. Located on Lower Johnson across from Market Square.

Oscar and Libby's
560 Johnson Street, 250 382 7279
www.oscarandlibbys.com
Tucked inside Market Square (Johnson Street side)... there are gift items, knick-knacks, jewelry, cool animal hat's and gloves, all that is weird, whacky & a wee bit whimsical...something for everybody.

Nest & Cradle
554 Yates Street, 250 384 6378
http://www.mynestandcradle.com/
You will want to live in this store. Offering goods in apothecary, housewares, furniture, clothing, accessories, jewelry, baby goods, books and paper products. They showcase several heritage brands, emerging labels, as well as local jewels that are a little newer to the game. It is modern, clean, and so stylish!

• PLAY

Market Square
http://www.marketsquare.ca/
Located between Johnson and Pandora between Wharf and Government Street, this is a neat little square edged with some great shopping. Hip Baby is on the Johnson Street side, and in the square top level is a fun knick knack/gag store Oscar & Libby's. There are a few restaurants and café's here, Mexi-Go, and Wanna Waffle. You can grab a bite and go down into the square to let your kids run around a bit. Sometimes there are event's here...but mostly it just a big empty car free area...perfect to let your little ones burn off some steam from shopping with you (lower Johnson has some of Victoria's best boutique shopping)!

Bastion Square
http://bastionsquare.ca/
Between Government and Wharf and Pandora and Yates is Bastion Square, another place the kids can bump around. While a little more busy then Market Square, and not so contained, you can still manage to have a coffee and let them roam around (while closely watched of course).

Empress Hotel
721 Government Street, 250 384 8111
http://www.fairmont.com/empress-victoria/
While probably not typically kid friendly, it is worth it
to at least walk through the Empress Hotel in Victoria's
Inner Harbour area (stop to use the restroom)...it is
opulent and lavish. It is reminiscent of an era gone by
and is quite a feast for the eyes.
If you happen to be visiting in December they have a
pretty fabulous collection of Christmas tree's.

China Town
On Fisgard Street between Government and Wharf
Street.
Victoria's China town (the oldest one in BC) is only a
block long and runs along Fisgard between Government
and Wharf. There are shops and some cafés along this
street. Make sure you walk down Fan Tan Alley- it is so
narrow you can reach out and touch both sides of the
wall!

The Atrium
On Blanshard Street between Johnson and Yates
Again, not a typical place to play, but with the shortages
of available child friendly spots in downtown, The Atrium
becomes a contender- especially as it is indoors, so it
becomes a perfect spot to wait out the rain.
It is a beautiful building; reclaimed wood, glass, concrete
and steel. Habit is here, as well as Pig and Zambris.
There is a relaxed hip vibe here, people coming and
going, sitting having coffee, or catching up on some
emails. Inside there is a skylight covered communal
courtyard where you can sit and let your kids walk
around somewhat unhindered.

• THE WESTSHORE

The Westshore- sounds like a cool beachy area, when in fact it is anything but that. Langford, which has been re-branded The Westshore, is Victoria's big box suburbs. Located 30 minutes outside of Victoria, it is home to most of Victoria's big box stores and a whole slew of new townhouse developments. So, if you like big box shopping, and want to drag the kids along, there are some family friendly things to do along the way.

As far as groceries go, your best bet is to go to the West Shore Town Center. There is a Fairway Market, BC Liquor Store, and a Shoppers Drug Mart spread throughout.

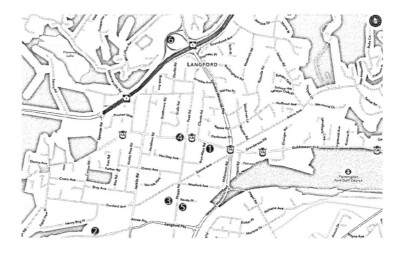

1. Tumblebums
   & Cafe Mexi-go
   & Bin 4
2. Eagleridge Community Center
3. Westshore Town Center
4. A to Z Kids Consignment
5. Pig BBQ
   & Superstore
6. Costco

• EAT

Pig BBQ Joint
129-2955 Phipps Road, 250 590 7627
http://pigbbqjoint.com/
Pig's second location is near the Westshore Town Center and Superstore. They offer finger lickin' bbq in a cool no nonsense counter service fashion. Pig is stroller friendly, has highchairs, and a kid's menu.

Café Mexi-go
735 Goldstream Ave, 250 391 4047
http://cafemexigo.com/
This is one of three locations. Café MexiGo is located in the same strip mall as Tumblebums and has quick counter service, high chairs, and can make simple fare for your little ones (think cheese quesadilla). The food is good, and there are definitely some healthy options.

Bin 4 Burger Lounge
102-716 Goldstream Avenue, 778 265 5464
http://www.bin4burgerlounge.com/
This sit down place offers burgers done in a hip way. Sometimes it can seem a little clubby, but the burgers are good. They choose local when they can, and the meat is all antibiotic free. There are highchairs, and kid's menus.
Bin 4 is in the same area as Tumblebums.

• SHOP

Western Speedway Swap and Shop
http://www.westernspeedway.net/
In the summer months there is a giant Flea Market at The Western Speedway. You feel like you are in an episode of American Gypsies when you go here- it is quite a spectacle, the people watching is amazing, and there is a lot of stuff here. A good place for a kid to fritter away their allowance- so if you are into this sort of thing, check it out.

Westshore TownCenter
2945 Jacklin Road, 250 474 3269
http://westshoretowncentre.com/
Here you will find Carters, Winners, and Jamtot's (a toy store), as well as Shoppers Drug Mart, Fairway's Market, and a Starbucks.

A-Z Kids Consignment
801 Goldstream Ave, 250-474-7769
A good assortment of kid's clothes and toys, plus a small selection of maternity wear.

Real Canadian Superstore
835 Langford Parkway, 250-391-3137
http://www.superstore.ca/
Across from the Westshore Town Center is the Superstore. While a grocery store, they also sell everything else you could need. Baby supplies, toys, cosmetics, and the clothing line Joe Fresh- which has some pretty stylish and affordable kid's clothes.

Costco
799 McCallum Rd, 250 391 1151
http://www.costco.ca/
If you are into Costco, it's in Langford.

• PLAY

Tumblebums
735 Goldstream Ave, 250 474 7529
http://www.tumblebums.com/
Mon to Sat 9-4
This is the place to go for really little kids- a big room filled with soft foam blocks, a pirate ship, a couple of slides, and lots of toys. Perfect for those from crawling to around 4. They have snacks and coffee for sale- and do not allow outside food and drink in.

They also have a wonderful toy store.

Bear Mountain Swimming Pool
1999 Country Club Way, 250 391 7160
http://bearmountain.ca/Fitness
For a drop in of $15 you can use the outdoor pool at the Westin. The pool here has a very resorty feel, and you get to lounge around the pool chairs and use nice fluffy white towels.
Walk over to one of the restaurants on the property and have a bite to eat afterwards.

Eagleridge Center
1089 Langford Parkway, 250.391.1738
http://www.eagleridgecentre.com/
Eagleridge Center is paydirt to kids. It houses Playzone, which is a huge indoor playground for kids walking to 8. They can climb up ladders, through tubes, and netting (all safely of course), and slide down big slides! There is a special area for toddlers and a parent zone too.
Also at the Eagleridge Center is mini golf, bowling, indoor and outdoor ice skating in the winter and a water park in the summer, as well as a foam ball shooting area! Eureka!

• SIDNEY

Sidney is around a half hour drive from Victoria. It is a neat little town with a 50's feel. You will see what I mean when you get there. The main drag has a bunch of little mom and pop stores, bakeries, and restaurants. There is a nice walkway down by the water and couple of playgrounds.
The main draws are The Shaw Ocean Discovery Center and The Sidney Night Market (in the summer).
Sidney is right off of the highway on the way out to the ferries, so you could always leave a little early if you are truly dying to see it. If you are feeling crunched for time, don't worry about seeing it though, the long drive out isn't really returned in amazing kid things.

Date night

There is a Safeway and a Thrifty Foods as soon as you exit from the highway.

• EAT

Maria's Souvlaki
9812 Second Street, 250 656 9944
Maria's is the place to go for Greek Food. It's nice and close to the pier, just off of the main drag on Second Street.   It is family run and they have quick counter service, high chairs, and colouring. Oh, yes, and great Greek food!!

Woodshed
103-2360 Beacon Avenue
http://www.woodshedsidney.com
Woodshed has a cozy warm room, and pretty good thin crust wood fired pizza.

Starbucks
2471 Beacon Ave, 250 665 0949
http://www.starbucks.ca/

• SHOP

Buddies Toys
2494 Beacon Ave, 250 655 7171
http://buddiestoys.ca/
Great selection of all sorts of toys! The staff is super helpful and friendly. Your kids won't want to leave!

The Gift Shop at Shaw Ocean Discovery Center
You hit this gift shop upon exiting the Discovery Center. They have a neat selection of ocean related educational toys and books.

• DATE NIGHT

So, you have begged borrowed and stole, and now you have a night out without kids. What to do? Where to go? Don't worry, there are some amazing places in Victoria where you can cozy up with your date and have a smashing time.

Brasserie L'ecole
1715 Government Street, 250 475 6260
http://www.lecole.ca

Brass (as the locals call it), is our favorite date night destination. The food (casual French) is always amazing. Think Steak & Frites, Mussels, Oysters, Trout and Green Beens. I could go on. It is all truly amazing. The service is bang on, and the room is small, crowded and lively. They do not take reservations and are VERY busy. I suggest going early (around 5:30), and putting your name on the list. Then you can go have a couple of drinks while you wait.

Veneto
1450 Douglas Street, 250 383 7310
http://www.venetodining.com

Housed in the Rialto Hotel, Veneto is a great place to go for drinks. They have an awe inspiring cocktail list. The room is modern and happening, and the food is not that bad either. This is a great place to go, if you are waiting for a table at Brasserie L'ecole or just want a drink.

Stage Wine Bar
1307 Gladstone Ave, 250 388 4222
http://stagewinebar.com

Tucked away in Fernwood, Stage is one of those great places that you wish was in your neighborhood. The food is amazing, all small plates, and all good. They have tons of different types of wine, and offer taster sizes, as well as full glasses. They take reservations for large groups early. If there is a wait, you can pop across the street to the Fernwood Inn for a drink.

Zambri's
820 Yates Street, 250 360 1171
http://www.zambris.ca
While it's fine to come here with your kids, it's extra fine to come here without them. The food is great (rustic Italian), the room is airy and modern, and the servers know their stuff. If you are feeling adventurous, trust your server to suggest wine to pair with your meal. They make magic happen. Zambri's does take reservations.

Vis a Vis- Wine and Charcuterie Bar
2232 Oak Bay Avenue, 230 590 7424
http://www.visavisoakbay.com
This tiny little Oak Bay hot spot has the most charming room ever. Obviously they have a great selection of charcuterie, but they also have lots of other tasty little morsels on offer. And of course wine. Lot's of wine. Call for reservations.

The London Chef
953 Fort Street, 250 590 1865
http://thelondonchef.com
Offering very fun and very interactive cooking classes, a night at The London Chef may not be a typical date night, but it can be all sorts of fun. You will get down and dirty in a kitchen you will wish was your own. Chef and Owner Dan Hayes does an amazing job of keeping things lively and teaching you wonderful things you can do with food. Check their web site for classes- things do tend to book up fast, so this one is worth planning ahead.

ulla
509 Fisgard Street, 250 590 8795
http://www.ulla.ca
All about local & all about technique. And all about good. That pretty much sums up ulla. If you are seeking a fine dining experience, then come to ulla. The room is warm and inviting, and the service is great. They also have a lovely selection of wine's and cocktails, and they take reservations.

The Tapa Bar
620 Trounce Ally, 250 383 0013
http://tapabar.ca
Giant pitchers of Sangria. Need I go on? If you want a casual fun night out pop in here. It is bustling, loud, and everything you want in a Tapa Bar. The food is good, and the sangria better! Call for reservations.

Ebizo Sushi
604 Broughton Street, 250 383 3234
If you are craving sushi, then Ebizo is the place to go. Try the Tuna Tataki. It will leave you thinking about for the rest of your life. It's that good. The room is by no means impressive, but the food makes up for that. Call for reservations.

• TRAVEL TIPS

Our family has done a fair amount of traveling. Before Baby Hank had turned one he had been to 5 different countries!

We find our best days are when we pick an activity that centers around our children, and then try to squeeze something good out of the surrounding areas for us. This might mean simply just making our way to a playground that we were lucky enough to hear about, but making sure we grab a perfectly made cappuccino along the way. After that we will try to source out a quick but tasty lunch, and then make our way back 'home' for a little down time (and a nap). After nap we usually make going to get dinner supplies the activity... and yes, that's it.

Trying to fit too much into a day makes for a cranky everybody, and it's not really worth it. If you keep things easy and relaxed and focus on finding a nice place to play you get to see more of the real city, not just jam packed tourist traps.

Travel Tips

Here is a list of travel tips that I find make things easier.

Packing

- We use packing cubes, they are a bit of investment, but they are worth it. Every family member gets their own 'cube' (a mini bag that fits into your suitcase). It makes packing, and finding things so easy. Plus your suitcase looks satisfyingly organized.
- I find it helpful to limit carry on bags. This way you do not have to keep track of so much. Here is what we bring on the plane. One carry-on sized wheelie suitcase and the diaper bag. That's it. Just put anything you will need on the plane into the wheelie suitcase, and when you get to your seat unpack. Take out the games and books and snacks and have it all handy, and then stow that suitcase up top. This makes not only keeping track of things easier, but it makes it easier on the plane if everything is out. Then you are not scrunching down and rooting around under the seat every three minutes.
- Unpack the baby-wipes, and have them handy. You will need them.
- We pack food tubes too- they are so convenient for both the little and bigger kids.
- Pack more snacks, diapers, and formula then you think you will need. We learned this the hard way, on a 5 hour delay.
- Pack a change of clothes in your carry on for your kids.
- Pack light- this is a hard one...but in the end it is you who will be lugging around all this stuff, and we all know that you will end up shopping wherever you are.

If you have a formula fed baby

- Pack (in the diaper bag) a thermos of heated water and then pack along a formula dispenser and bottles. Just let them know at security that you have this stuff and that it is for your baby. They may check the water, but they will let you through. Then when you are in the air you are not trying to get bottles warmed, it is all just there at your finger tips.

At the Airport and on the Plane

- Arrive early! You just never know what will happen, and rushing is the worst.
- Deep breaths at security. If the person behind you is eye rolling and being generally grumpy because you and your kids are in front of them- slow down...that will show them! Basically, just don't let the stress get to you. It is what it is, and you can only get you and your kids and your stroller and your everything through so quickly.
- If you are making a long trip- red eye is the way to go. Your kids will most likely sleep and you will not have to entertain them in 2 square feet for 8 hours.
- For older children bring along a compact game that they are into. We found UNO worked wonders.
- Invest is some child size earphones. They will make everything to do with in-flight entertainment less frustrating.

Flying with a lap baby

- We brought along a nursing pillow. My Breast Friend makes an inflatable one so it won't take up much room in your luggage. It gives a nice surface for a smaller baby to sleep on.

- If your plane is not full (check before you go to the airport), bring your carseat. They will usually let you have an extra seat if there is one available, and a baby in a car seat is way better then a baby on lap. I usually would try to book our seats with an empty on between us, hoping that someone wouldn't book a middle seat. It worked and we ending up with an extra seat. Obviously this is not a guarantee, but if it works you will be very thankful!
- Also bring along a carrier. It is very helpful at boarding and de planning to have your hands free. Plus your baby can sleep in it to. Ergo makes a travel carrier that rolls up compactly.

At your Destination
- As mentioned, I highly recommend getting a vacation rental or a place on airbnb.com. This way you are not stuck in one room with your kids. You have more room to spread out, and you can book a place that has toys! New toys will always keep kids occupied for a while- leaving you with some of your own time (hello wine & internet). Better yet do a House Swap. Then it's all free!
- Research the area you are staying. In Paris we stayed way too far from everything. This meant a ten minute walk to the metro, plus a twenty minute metro ride...this is too far and left a bad mark our trip. It is worth it to pay a little more and stay in a great area.
- Get recommendations from people who have been where you are going- especially if they went with their little ones. Then you will know where all the cool places that will work for you and your family are. You won't be wasting valuable time searching them out.
- Don't cram too much in. Your kids won't like it, and then in turn, neither will you. Do one main thing a day, then go the park, have a picnic, hang out in your nice place your painstakingly chose, and relax. Everyone will be happier!

- A place with a pool is a god send. Especially if your Husband/Travel Partner will play with the kids in the water all day while you swan around eating chips and reading your book!
- Bring a good quality travel stroller. We brought a really crappy sit and stand (Hudson does better on long days if he doesn't have to walk for hours). It was heavy and hard to push on the cobbled streets of Europe. Maybe if we had been at Disneyland it would have been ok. In hindsight I would have brought our good stroller from home with the little standing board on the back. Just think about where you are going. You may be up against bad strolling conditions...so you want your stroller to be up to the task.
- Know where the hospital or clinic is and have a bit of an emergency plan. You never know.

....

I hope this has given you every resource possible to plan and enjoy an amazing trip with your family.
I was inspired to write this book after countless trips with my little family. If I could find a blog or a book that outlined the areas we were visiting in a kid-centric way, my day was made.

Please note that as most of the business' I recommend are independents and that means that things can change quickly. I may mention pizza on Sundays, but by the time you arrive here, Sunday is now bagel day. It is best to call ahead or check their website to confirm. As for the maps you see, please do not use them as your bible. They are accurate, but not to the square foot. They are meant to show you the lay of the land, and what is close to what. This will help you in planning your day.

....